Finding your own way

Personal meditations for peace and balance.

by

Patrick W Kavanagh

Art by Bill Oliver

Copyright 2015 Patrick W Kavanagh

Dedicated to David H Nundy

for his friendship, compassion and kindness.

He will always be in our hearts,

Forward

Sadly, the western world has passed from the strict regimes of the Victorian age to the illusory freedoms of the twenty-first century, without any real improvement in the mental health or happiness of the majority of people. Many have left the repressive atmosphere of mainstream religions, only to fall prey to either excessive consumerism or the petty tyranny of gurus and groups who demand much more than was ever asked of our parents. We are bombarded day and night by those who would use our need for meaning in our lives, to sell us an endless succession of ideologies or distractions. It is getting harder to know who to believe.

True balance and happiness come from seeing and understanding our own individual needs and learning to gauge when it is appropriate to satisfy them, and how best to do so.

Much of what we do is controlled by fears and wishes, which are just below our normal level of awareness. Most of our feelings of isolation and insecurity come from our inability to gain contact with this important part of our total personality. So too, do many of our aches, pains and illnesses.

Most attempts at dealing with our psyche come from various ideologies and schools of psychology.

Each tries to sell us their own world-view as part of their treatment. For those who are desperate and unable to cope, losing a part of our individuality is probably a reasonable exchange.

However, for those of us who are coping, but wish for a calmer, more peaceful, and a more successful and meaningful life, - the time has come to learn how to bring a feeling of connectedness back into our worlds.

In this book, I offer some simple techniques and meditations for those who wish to open up to their own inner world and find a fresh perspective, that is theirs alone. Despite their simplicity, these techniques are very powerful. The first basic relaxation exercise cured a lifelong speech impediment at the age of nineteen. Beforehand, I could never complete a single sentence or even say my own name. Since then I have worked as a shop manager, a salesman, a telephone counsellor and have made many public addresses including presenting my own poetry at a venue in Covent Gardens, London.

Meditation does not take hours of effort or need the torture of holding uncomfortable positions.

A chair, a couch, or a bed in a quiet room is all that is needed.

Many will find the benefits of meditation to be evident after a very short time, - they will feel calmer, more relaxed and have a greater sense of well-being.

In the longer term, many may find that they are finally prepared to make positive life-changes, or discover a new creativity, increased intuition, and a fresh sense of connectedness with the world.

There are challenges to be met for those who wish to make greater changes to their lives.

Seeing ourselves more clearly is not always a comfortable experience.

For that reason, Bill and I have prepared artwork and poetry that will act as rough guides to help set boundaries and allow the reader to select which areas they wish to explore on their personal inner journeys. Simply glance through the book until you find a topic you wish to explore, - or a text or picture which resonates with you at a time. Then allow yourself to become absorbed in the imagery before meditating.

Those readers who do not visualise easily will also find this very useful.

Patrick W Kavanagh and Bill Oliver,

21/11/2015

Chapter 1 Basic Relaxation techniques

Chapter 2 First Steps

Chapter 3 Acceptance

Chapter4 Western Meditation Techniques

Chapter 5 Setting Boundaries

Chapter 6 The Third Eye Meditation

Chapter 7 Meditating with a Spirit Drum

Chapter 8 The Shamanistic Path

Chapter 9 Candle Meditation

Chapter 10 Seeking Our inner child-

Chapter 11 Finding Joy

Chapter 12 The Journey

Chapter 13 Challenging Times.

Chapter 14 Finding Love

Chapter 15 The Muse Awaits

Chapter 16 About the Author.

Chapter 1

Basic relaxation

Relax!

A certain amount of tension is necessary for our lives. In fact, it is essential! Life requires tension, - as does every enjoyable activity which we can indulge in. There is a joy in handling even simple everyday tasks. There is a sense of achievement in pushing the limits of our strength, speed and endurance.

Even fear can be positive. It prepares us for action and helps us to think faster and act decisively in a crisis. Then, we relax. Everything rests and we return to a normal level of tension.

Or, at least we should.

Many of us don't. We live in fear. What will my partner say if I work late again? What will my boss do if I do not finish this job in time? What if I fail this exam? What if I cannot pay my bills?

Childhood fears remain below the level of awareness. For some, the fear of hell-fire, or, perhaps separation or maybe the bogeyman that we imagined to be under the bed.

Unexamined childhood fears and traumas cause much of our feeling of unease and feed our tendency to worry about the future. I have noticed that people often feel an emotion first, and then, look around them for a cause to ascribe it to later. We justify our feelings by blaming the people and situations around us. As a result, we cannot fully trust our own judgement until we learn to relax and become more aware of our own habitual feelings.

This first exercise is probably the longest one in the book, - but it quickly becomes streamlined with practice. Just by learning to relax for a short period, we can begin to realise what a normal level of tension should be. Regular practice will quickly allow us to relax at our own command.

The effects are far-reaching, - allowing us to gain control of many situations in which we were previously at the mercy of our emotions, and the manipulation of others. It is also the first step in effective meditation.

Basic Relaxation

This exercise is best carried out, initially, in a lying down position. With practice, it can then be done sitting down. After a while, the reader will be able to relax totally in most situations with a single simple command to relax. A walk in the woods can become a healing meditation.

In the first attempts at relaxing, there is a risk that the reader may fall into a deep, healing sleep.

Make sure that there are no candles burning, or anything that may become a hazard should you do so. Also make sure that you are warm, comfortable and are not going to be disturbed. Turn off your mobile phone and inform anyone in the house that you are unavailable for a while. Wear loose comfortable clothing. Lie flat on your back in a comfortable place. Feel free to use a pillow if it is more comfortable.

Take a deep breath.

As you breathe in, tense your whole body.

Breathe out and say "Relax" in your mind as you let go of the tension.

Breathe in and tense..... Breathe out and relax.

Breathe in and tense ….. Breathe out and relax.

Repeat this a few more times. Each time, tell yourself to "Relax!"

Allow yourself to breathe slowly and easily

Now turn your attention to your body, starting at your toes.

Wriggle your toes and tense them. Then tell them to relax as you let go of the tension.

Then relax your feet. First one foot, then the other foot, then both feet at the same time.

Tense and relax.

Then you calves, each one, then both. Then tense from the tip of your toes to your calves and relax.

Work your way up to your thighs. Tense and relax.

Again, become aware of your body from your toes to your thighs and tell yourself to "relax!"

Work your way up your torso. Tense and relax.

Then up to your shoulders and down your arms.

Wriggle your fingers, then tense and relax.

Pay careful attention to your neck muscles. Tense and relax.

Then the back of your head, tense and relax.

Then become aware of your facial muscles. Tense and relax.

Then focus on your forehead and the top of your head.

Take a deep breath and tense your whole body.

Then, as you exhale say "Relax!"

Just let everything go.

By this time you should feel very heavy as if you were melting into the surface beneath you.

Repeat a few times, depending on the time available.

This simple exercise often results in discovering hidden attitudes and fears which are held in the muscles as "memories". It does this by releasing the habitual tension that holds the energies in place in our bodies. Regular practice can loosen the grip of unconscious negative expectations on our health and interactions with others. I would recommend keeping a diary and noting any dreams or reveries as well as day to day events. I would also recommend practising this until it becomes streamlined, before moving on to any of the other meditations.

Chapter 2

First Steps

What is most urgently needed, in these hectic days is peace and calm. Meditation is not the difficult task that it is often made out to be, - so, for this first exercise, we will use the relaxation technique as a stepping off point. Tense and relax a few times then read the poem and spend some time in looking at the image, before beginning the relaxation technique. After you have totally relaxed, simply allow yourself to remember the images and the moods associated with them. Let them flow through your mind without any judgement or analysis. Do not worry if you fall asleep and miss this step. You will have begun the work as you rested and healed. You can always return to this section after mastering more advanced techniques.

A meditation for seeking calm and meaning in our lives.

A Rose in Sunlight

A ray of sunlight, glancing briefly through the trees, dazzles a solitary, pale, blue rose.

Fragile petals kiss the frost before her sleeping sisters have arose

Scattered on a deep green bush and nestled safely in their buds,

they wait for warmer days, while she has rushed ahead.

She sheds a single dew-drop tear, for beauty all too soon to fade,

Before the summer comes to pass, her pretty petals will be shed.

Weep not, sister rose,

Your beauty has not passed unseen.

For, all too soon, we both are destined to return

to where, deep in our hearts, we've always been.

Back to that place, for which our spirit yearns,

where hunger never bites, nor desert burns.

Chapter 3

Acceptance

The hardest lesson that we need to earn as human beings is acceptance. It is not a vague feeling of goodwill, nor a sign of weakness and vacillation. It is a powerful tool for opening up our intuition and creativity. It gives us new insights and new options in many situations. It allows us to take a realistic and honest look at situations in our homes and at work and at many social events.

Where once we may have been victims of our own emotions and impulses, we begin to gain the ability to take control of situations around us. It is the key to unlocking a positive future.

As we learn to accept others without judgement, we learn to open up to our own inner worlds.

We learn to see ourselves honestly and without self-criticism. We can then begin to see, and deal with, our own hidden motivations and develop true spontaneity. To encourage acceptance, we need to release ourselves from our need for certainty. Remember, it is inconceivable, that we are always right and others are always wrong. This simple truth is a good starting point.

I cannot emphasise enough how important a force like acceptance will become in our lives.

It is a key element in self-healing. It is essential for any true learning and personal development.

It is best to use a comfortable chair at this stage, to lessen the likelihood of falling asleep.

Again, just read the text and muse over the images. Then, allow the images and ideas to flow through your mind unchallenged, both during and after the deep relaxation technique.

If you wish, you can now begin to add some visualisation techniques.

If your eyes open, just allow them to close again after a few moments.

As you breathe in, imagine a stream of golden light flowing down into your body from above.

As you breathe out, imagine it flowing out from your torso and forming a golden ball around you.

Repeat this a few times and return to your musings.

You may repeat the sequence a few times if you wish.

Allow yourself time to return to normal consciousness before driving or operating any machinery.

A drink and a snack is a good way to return fully to normal waking consciousness.

Be aware that time distortion often occurs during meditations. An hour may pass in what feels like a few moments, or time may seem to stretch and a short session may seem to last much longer.

This section will ease your journey into later, more advanced, meditations.

Try not to rush ahead or work to any targets. The journey is what counts. Every single moment has its own unique value. This is your journey and will unfold in your own unique way. You will discover a wisdom and guidance that will benefit you for your whole life as you begin to discover your own inner resources.

Certainty

Like a suit of armour,

Polished gold that gleams and sparkles in the light.

That Blessed Shield that keeps our ego safe.

No nagging doubts disturb us in the night.

No second thoughts to make our conscience chafe.

The Joy of never being wrong,

Those great eternal truths that beam down from above.

Our principles that keep us different from the milling throng.

When we love Certainty,

Its charms can keep us safe from any other love.

We feel misunderstood by those who do not truly Know.

Their dreadful ignorance and anarchy surround us every day.

If only we could set them on the path they need to go.

If only they could understand the things we try to say,

Then we could let them bask in our enlightened glow.

But then,

How can I teach the sparrow how to fly?

They seemed to know just what to do,

Before I ever had a chance to teach them how.

I often watch in envy as they dance and weave beneath the evening sky.

The crimson setting sun, that lights their antics, lights the furrows on my brow.

Streaking red and gold across the purple hills and dark green fields,

Its rainbow glory blinds my eyes and lets me see,

This world was doing fine before there ever was a Me.

Once we start to meditate, we open a doorway to our unconscious thoughts and feelings. This may not always be a comfortable experience. Take things slowly. If you become unhappy with the experience stop and open your eyes. If you feel tearful for no apparent reason, do not worry. It is simply a release of energy. But if you find yourself becoming moody or unhappy, - just take a break for a few days. This will give you time to assimilate whatever is being released from your unconscious mind. This is a very personal journey, and a lot of the images that will flow into your mind may seem strange at first, - but they will tend to have a relevance to your life which will become clear in time.

Many of the images may even seem religious. This is because they are a part of our human history and have been experienced and interpreted by many people over the ages. It is your own personal reaction to the images which is important. You will come across them in the guided meditations also. Again this is because we all share many of these ancient images as part of our common heritage. As you learn to deal with these ancient images, you will come to realise that they can release energy into our lives. This is not a religious exercise. Meditation on these symbols will allow us to tap into skills and abilities and attributes that are dormant in our minds, - regardless of whether we are atheists, agnostics or members of any of the mainstream religions. Our journey is about finding balance in our lives between our inner and outer needs but doing it in our own unique way.

Chapter 4

Western meditation techniques

There are thousands of books on eastern meditation, but I wish to concentrate on the western traditions as they are less well documented, and require much less time to master. These traditions have been hidden for hundreds of years until the early nineteen hundreds. Some were the sole province of the religious orders and others were carried on in secret, by various groups and individuals.

Although the reasoning behind the various systems may seem flawed to the modern mind, I can assure the reader that these exercises work. My own belief is that these were discovered by trial and error and whichever techniques worked were passed down to others, enmeshed in whatever ideology suited the teacher. Also, I have found, through personal experience, that there is a huge fund of knowledge within the collective unconscious mind (Carl Jung) that we can tap into during dreams and meditations.

The Treeing Exercise

This is a well-known meditation and it covers an important area of western tradition.

It helps us increase our feeling of 'connectedness' with the earth and gives us greater control over our altered states of mind as we journey. It is always a good idea to begin any meditations with the treeing exercise. As the name suggests, it helps us anchor ourselves emotionally before exploring our inner worlds. It also gives a great feeling of calm energy and optimism. This can be used anywhere, either sitting, standing or lying down. Sitting against a large mature tree during this meditation will certainly add to its effects.

Close your eyes and breathe as slowly, and as deeply as is comfortable.

Imagine that you are a tree.

Visualise the sun above you pouring light and warmth onto your crown and branches.

Feel the warmth flowing through you and down into your legs and feet.

Picture your body filling with bright light.

Imagine your feet are rooted to the ground.

In your mind see the light form tendrils which push deep into the earth, like the roots of a tree.

Push the tendrils deep into the earth as the energy of the sun pours through your body.

See the tendrils spread out into tiny roots and anchor firmly into the soil.

Now, as you breathe in, draw the light of the sun down your spine and deep into the earth.

As you breathe out, draw the energies of the earth up through your roots, along your spine, and through the top of our head... sending their vibration through your body and out to the universe.

As you breathe in, feel the light flowing down into the ground and clearing and tension and pain from your body and into the earth to be transformed and healed.

When you feel totally relaxed and energised, then you may continue on to another meditation, or slowly open your eyes when you feel ready to do so.

Seeking Peace in a Garden of Roses.

Morning sunlight sparkling on a single drop of dew,

Light cascades like a rainbow on a rose.

Toes curling on the cool, wet grass.

The world is still asleep.

You walk in solitary silence, but you are not alone.

You share your thoughts and cares with One who truly Knows.

The One whose Spirit warms your blood and fills your heart.

The One who pours Their love into your very bones.

And you are blessed.

Memories come back to you unbidden,

Happy times that filled your heart with joy.

The chattering of your brain is stilled,

The worries and the sorrows drift away.

Then slowly, gently you become aware of now,

You face the world without the needless furrows on your brow.

And you are blessed.

Touch the rose with tenderness,

Kiss it gently as you taste the dew upon your lips.

Breathe in deeply as you fill your lungs with beauty.

Taste the fragrance of the morning garden,

Heady with the scent of earth and grass and summer flowers.

Stretch and raise your hands up to the sky,

and know that you are blessed.

This is an ideal meditation to follow the 'treeing' exercise. It can bring a feeling of relaxation, expansiveness, and connection to nature. It will increase our feelings of calm and inner peace.

Sometimes we are not ready to face our feelings head-on. Perhaps we have been under a lot of strain and feel tired and depleted. Too many demands from life may have left us feeling drained and 'empty'. Issues with friends and family that we have avoided dealing with may have exhausted our energy, - leaving us in no fit state to deal with them. Be gentle with yourself. We all hide away from things that are too painful to deal with. Simply take the time to heal and regroup your energies before tackling difficult issues.

We sometimes need to take the time to rest and nurture ourselves. Sadly, it is not always possible to take the time needed to do this. Use this meditation to take your own personal "mini-break" when you get a few spare minutes.

Breathe deeply and relax as you exhale a few times. Then take a few minutes to absorb the poem and gaze at the picture. Then use the relaxation exercise or one of the other meditations in the book, and allow your mind to take you to a pleasant safe place where you will find inner healing and often, wisdom and guidance.

Chapter 5

Setting Boundaries.

Not every adult believes in the existence of the spirit worlds, but almost every child does.

That we still have that child within us and are influenced by forgotten beliefs, has a major impact on the results of our meditation. If we wish to ensure that our journeys are positive and uplifting, it is best to set boundaries before we begin. The poems and art in this book will naturally tend to lead to the areas mentioned and always have a positive aspect. However, as we forge our own path to mental and emotional balance, it is best to have this ability completely under our own control.

Keep an open mind about the imagery and words used. This is not a book which favours any belief system. I have witnessed many different beliefs helping people who needed that particular change of perspective at that point in their lives. I am a pragmatist. I have only included those things which I know to be helpful. I leave it to others to argue as much as they wish about "absolute truth".

What is important to us as individuals is to build a better relationship with our total selves. Learning to trust ourselves can be a difficult task for some. If we start with what we know is true in our own experience we can slowly build on this as we grow and develop.

If prayer has worked in the past, then pray for wisdom and guidance. I can guarantee from personal experience that you will be shown a way forward. If you are non-religious, then sit down and ask your subconscious mind to cooperate in finding a better way to life and a more useful way to see life. You will find that as you open to your own inner creativity, then many paths will open for you. All you need to do is to stipulate that only those learnings for which you are ready will be given to you.

The Auric Egg

This exercise has many applications apart from setting boundaries during meditation.

It will help the reader in stressful situations and in dealing with those who would try to overpower our emotions and sensitivities. Once mastered, I would advise using it in any situation in which we feel anxious or threatened.

I once had a student who believed he had to enter some type of bird's egg and complained about the yoke being in his way, so I will try to describe the auric egg in as great a detail as possible.

Before you start the exercise, take a peek at a fine mesh colander or a flour sieve.

Try to picture the fine mesh in the shape of an egg with the wide part at the bottom. If you find it easier to do so, - just imagine it as a sphere around you.

It is best to start this meditation with the treeing exercise. (section 5)

Feel the light from the sun pouring in through the crown of your head.

As you picture the light from the sun filling your body, begin to push it out from your solar plexus.

As you breathe in, push the light out until it forms the shape of an egg around your body.

See the light turn to gold and form a shell around you made from fine golden filaments.

Tell yourself that this light will let nothing negative or dark enter your mind. Only positive thoughts and feelings are allowed through it. All else is filtered out.

Take your time. Spend as long as you need to master this.

If you have trouble in visualising, then think of yourself in a warm, safe bubble. Feel the warmth around you. Tell yourself that you are loved and protected.

If there are any smells or sounds that you associate with comfort and safety, then take the time to remember them.

Remember... there is no rush and no pressure. It may take a few attempts for some people to get this exercise flowing smoothly.

Was there a special place where you felt safe? Remember that.

Was there someone in your childhood who was a protector? Remember them. Say their name. Remember how you felt when they were around. Fictional characters will work too!

Even if you visualise well, adding these memories will make what you are doing easier and even more effective in setting a safe boundary for your meditations.

Then allow your mind to wander.

Now might be a good time to start keeping a record of your thoughts and feelings.

Paint the Sky with Summers Hues

Paint the sky with deepest blue,

Paint your world with all the brightest colours and the lightest hues,

Golden corn and buttercups, a gleaming yellow sun,

Silver streams that sparkle, - cool and clean as when the world began.

Sweet green grass and roses of the deepest red,

Shady fern-filled forests with the softest, mossy pillows where you rest your weary head.

Why imagine gloom and doom,

when you can paint your future with your brightest hopes instead.

The ocean beckons us with promises of warm dry sand that trickles through our hands,

A bucket and a spade create a faery castle or a soldier's keep with turrets and a moat.

The simple joy of lying on the beach and listening to the waves,

and making love hearts on the sand, which wash away as quickly as we write.

Long mild days to trek, to travel, to explore,

or lay and bask; - I dare to question, who could ask for more,

The heaviest of hearts can find that on a summer's day it lifts.

The rich and poor alike can both enjoy the summer's gifts.

Summer is a season and a place within your heart.

Summer lasts forever when our final winter thaws,

Even in this fleeting, fickle world of pain and flaws,

Summer is the journey of a heart that needs no laws.

Summer is that secret place of calm within the storm,

Summer is the goal of those who seek to live beyond the norm,

Even as the icy grip of winter howls, and swirls around our homes,

Summer is the warmth inside our hearts, and hope of better things to come.

Just take a few minutes to absorb the images from the text and the art.

This meditation will help boost optimism and courage. It will help us to see beyond present difficulties and start to manifest more positive and helpful responses to challenging situations. Nothing material lasts forever in this fleeting world, especially not hardship or misfortune. What does last are the valuable lessons that we learn, and the joy in our hearts from happy times. The wheel of life will turn. Winter thaws into spring and then the summer comes.

Now is the time to remember all the good in your life and all the times that you felt loved and protected. This will help to release the energy from your subconscious mind and free you to find the best solutions to any obstacles in your journey to a happier and more balanced life.

Take the time to compile a short list of your successes in the past and present. Remember books and films where the main character won through after many difficulties. Concentrate on the positive things in your life and only on actions you can perform immediately to help the situation. Then tell yourself that you have done all you can for the moment and relax until a solution comes to you from within.

Chapter 6

The Third Eye Meditation.

The 'third eye' is positioned behind the forehead just above the bridge of the nose and connects to both halves of the brain. Believed by Rene Descartes to be the seat of the soul, it is widely written about in eastern and in 'new age' philosophies. It has strong links with sleep, hibernation, libido and ageing. It is believed by many to be a doorway for astral travel to the inner and spiritual worlds.

An interesting fact to consider is that blue light and modern electric lights reduce the effectiveness of the pineal gland and interfere with sleep patterns.

Red light, - such as candlelight and firelight have no such effect.

Whether we believe astral travel to be a journey to different worlds, or simply an imaginative exercise, has little bearing on its effectiveness. Meditating on the third eye increases our use of intuition and allows us to access guidance and wisdom in the form of many different archetypal figures from our unconscious mind. I know from experience that this wisdom exists and can be tapped by meditation. I will leave the decision on its ultimate source for the reader to make.

Third Eye Meditation.

Relax, close your eyes, and breathe as slowly and as deeply as is comfortable, in a dim room.

Candlelight or a dim red light is best for this exercise.

Breathe in golden light through the crown of your head and push it deep into the earth.

Imagine it drawing down any tension and worries into the earth as you breathe.

Create a sphere of golden light around your body, encased in a mesh of fine golden filaments.

Remind yourself that it is protecting you and allowing only positive influences to enter your mind during meditation.

As you breathe in, imagine your body filling with golden light.

As you breathe out, imagine it flowing out from you at a point just above and between both eyes.

Breathe in from the crown of your head and allow the golden light to flow through you down to the earth.

Breathe out through the third eye and become aware of it slowly opening.

Soon you will become aware of colours and a feeling of deep relaxation.

Take note of any other sounds, smells or sensations.

At this stage, many see a tunnel stretching out from their forehead.

If you are ready to journey, then think of a person or place that you wish to visit.

Allow yourself to be drawn through the tunnel and be aware of anything you experience in a calm, relaxed and non-judgemental manner. Simply allow the images and sensations to flow.

If you are not ready to journey yet, then simply continue the meditation for a while and take note of any images that come into your mind.

If you drift into sleep, then be sure to write down anything which you can recall later. If you had a question, then the answer may well be in any dreams you have during your meditation or over the next couple of days. Also be aware of any 'coincidences' that occur after asking a specific question.

You may well receive your answer in apparently random comments by friends or on the media.

Portal Worlds.

Cold still waters.

A silver sheen to azure depths that mixed the oceans and the sky within the endless vault.

Stony heights of iridescent blue stretched up into eternity, beyond my visions reach.

It seemed as if I stood upon the threshold to a million worlds,

Which somehow hid within the bowels of the earth.

Apprehension gripped me,

As I paused to choose the path ahead and gauge the measure of my visions worth.

Not one path seemed easy to ascend,

Nor could I be sure, - what waited for me at my journeys end.

I stood perplexed, - my feet as frozen as my will.

I could not choose, but yet I must!

And let the journey be just what it will.

The time has come to learn to be,

the very best I may yet be.

I seek the guidance of the higher worlds.

I seek to turn the grit of life,

Into the beauty of sweet Wisdom's pearls.

I felt my guardian angels touch, and I was lifted up.

My heart rejoiced that I was not alone.

As we flew up to the heights, all sorrow fell away,

And in her loving arms, she carried me back home.

Was this a vision, or a memory or another life,-

I cannot really say.

For as we rose into the distant lights,

We left behind the tiresome thoughts, I carry through the day.

We may travel to many places, past, present and future when using the third eye meditation.

Try to always take note of your visions and experiences for later reference.

What is experienced will vary greatly from person to person and on every journey.

Make a point of alternating with a basic relaxation technique in order to allow yourself time to assimilate your experience.

It may take a while to become effective in using this visualisation. Do not assume that it has not worked, - if you either fall asleep or have simply had a calm soothing experience.

You may also confuse yourself by constantly repeating the exercise without giving yourself enough time for the information requested to become known to you by various means outside of your meditation period.

In the rare event of having a disturbing experience, simply open your eyes and slowly return to normal consciousness. Have a drink and a snack. Take a break for a few days and then keep to the basic relaxation exercise until you feel ready to travel again.

Developing our own path takes time, and nothing will come to us before we are ready for it.

Just approach these meditations in a relaxed easy-going manner and you will gain great benefits from them in a surprisingly short period of time.

Chapter 7

Meditating with a spirit drum.

One of the easiest and most effective ways to meditate is by using a 'spirit' drum.

Having been a part of many workshops and drumming circles, I can personally attest to the simplicity and effectiveness of using 'spirit' drums for healing and journeying.

If you have a few interested friends and somewhere to go to practice, - you will find that it is an amazing and uplifting experience.

Should you wish to form a circle, you will find that spirit drums vary greatly in price.

A lot of people use 'bodhrans' instead, as they are cheaper and can be bought from most music shops. They are hand drums used in traditional Irish and Celtic music.

If you look online, there are many useful videos to get you started. Compact discs are also widely available with shamanistic drumming and Spirit music. I would recommend Native American drumming tracks, but that is just a matter of personal taste, - there are drumming tracks available from many cultures.

If you decide to drum in a group, the biggest obstacle to success will be your own self-consciousness. Having just a small group of two or three close friends will help.

The rewards of overcoming your initial feelings of reserve are well worth the effort.

In a drumming circle, the energy of the drums take over, and the rhythm takes on a collective life of its own.

It is always a good idea to set out your intentions before drumming. Whether you wish to feel uplifted, journey, or send healing to someone, - make your intentions clear before beginning the drumming session. Imagine yourself working within a golden circle of love and protection.

Upload a few tracks online until you find a beat that appeals to you and practice it quietly in private until you feel confident with it. There is no great art or skill required. The most powerful beat is a simple steady rhythm of single beats on the drum. This is called a shamanistic beat.

Spirit Drum Meditation

To begin, choose a quiet area where you will be undisturbed.

Take several deep breaths and tell yourself to relax.

Take a little time to read the poem below and to absorb the images from the artwork

You may play a drumming track quietly in the background if you wish, but it is not essential.

Imagine a golden sphere of protection around you as you work.

Begin with the third eye meditation.

As you breathe out through your third eye, visualise a shining path ahead of you.

Allow yourself to be drawn onto this path.

You can see a fire ahead of you, in the distance, and you walk slowly towards it.

If you see any creatures nearby, take note, as they may be important to you later on in your journeys.

You will see a group of figures around the fire. Some may be drumming. Some may be dancing. How they appear to you will depend on what it is you need to learn on your path.

Spend some time by the fire and take note of whatever you experience there.

Stay near the fire until you are ready to return.

Turn back and walk down the path and you will find yourself back where you started the meditation. Breathe slowly and easily and open your eyes when you are ready.

If you feel uncomfortable at any stage of the exercise, simply open your eyes and you will return to your room, safe within the circle of light.

Finish the meditation by thanking your subconscious mind for its cooperation. Also, thank any Deities and helpers. Then draw the golden circle back to you and close the session.

What you experience and where you go on this journey will vary greatly according to your personal needs. It is always helpful to spend a few moments in setting the boundaries for your journey before you begin. What is it that you wish to achieve? What type of journey are you expecting? Is there some challenge or personal goal that you wish to focus on?

This meditation is particularly powerful when done in a drumming circle.

Be sure to have a drink and a snack before travelling home or handling any machinery.

Write down anything you saw, heard or felt. Especially, note any creatures that you encountered.

Drumbeats

The drums are beating softly in the distance,

Like a peaceful heart. they draw me to them,

leaving life's conundrums far behind.

Like poetry, with inspirations, much too large for words,

The rhythm opens up my soul and fills my mind.

As I sit and write, the rhythm of the drums still beats within my heart.

In the forest of my mind, I see the shamans dance and whirl.

Orange flames that go so high, they almost reach the moonlit sky.

Somewhere in the Once, or in the Now, they beat their drums for me.

And now the healing magic of their chants is reaching out to me.

Wolves with emerald eyes are in the shadows.

I can hear the eagles piercing cry.

Brother Bear is everywhere, and I can also see.

All the spirits of the native forest watching over me.

Lending me their powers, so I can live the life I never thought could be.

Poetry in every beat, and magic in the rhythm of the drums.

Through the cadence of his chants, I find the link, the shaman comes.

Healing for the body, for the spirit and the mind,

As I leave this world of consternation far behind,

and find again, the wisdom and the beauty that was meant for all mankind.

This is another meditation for the spirit drum which came to me a few years ago.

It is almost impossible to meditate without finding a great connectedness with the wider universe and the earth around us. This poem is a warning about the way we are treating the earth.

We are all interdependent, - if a single species dies, then we are all so much poorer and so is the legacy that we leave to our children. If the earth dies, - then we die with her.

Whether we have one life or many, we have a duty of care for the planet and those around us.

As we develop through meditation we will feel this much more keenly.

Reaching out to the world and the people, plants and animals around us will bring us much joy.

However, our increased sensitivity brings with it a need to learn to protect ourselves, and a tendency to avoid certain people and situations. Unexpected changes will begin to happen in our lives, as we move into areas of activity that were once difficult to even imagine.

Be prepared too, for resistance from family and friends as you move away from old habits and develop new areas of activity. Much of it will be in a misguided spirit of over-protection, so be patient in your dealings with those who fear the changes in your life will begin to balance out as you forge a new agreement with your subconscious mind. You will be forging a new path in life which is based on your own needs and not the expectations of others.

A Warriors Tears.

What will we make of the world when the last rose has died?

When all alone we stand upon the naked earth where once the weeping willow cried.

Where once the sparrow chirped upon the leafy bough,

And now, across the barren wastes, the wind blows soft and low

And when our world has gone,

Where will we go?

Where vast majestic rivers flowed, now runs a ragged little stream.

No fish still swim within its dark and murky flow.

No dragonflies above the bare, baked clay that guides its weary way.

No butterflies delight our eyes with a colourful display.

And when our world has gone,

Where will we go?

Take the seeds of mother earth and scatter them wherever you may go.

We can plant ten trees for every tree that dies.

Cut the fences, chop the posts and let the buffalo run free.

Take the earth back from the greedy; let us share it as we did in days of old.

For when our Mother dies,

Where will we go?

I channelled this in a couple of minutes. The first two verses came in an instant. I added the last verse after a moment's reflection as a reminder that there is always hope.

For those who drum, it chants well to a basic shamanistic beat or, "drums across the water" (such as you might hear in an old cowboy movie)

My wife, Tina, told me to sing it, and I grabbed my drum.

To my amazement, it just flowed through me. It was a very powerful experience.

Chapter 8

The Shamanistic Path

I add this section for those who are interested in the spiritualistic or shamanistic aspect of meditation. This is simply an introduction to the world of the shaman. For those who wish to delve further, I would advise finding a reliable teacher to help them. In the last twenty years, there has been a widening of interest in the healing and spiritual practices of our ancestors and many have found a pathway back to a more earth-centred method of teaching and healing.

As always, trust your own instincts. Find out as much as you can before becoming too closely involved with any particular individual. We all go through challenging times, - but if this person is not handling the important aspects of their lives very well, then perhaps they are not for you.

If they care more about money than the work they are doing, then they are most likely not the right person to teach you. If they take on too many students, then they may not be able to give the support needed. Many shamans offer healing and counselling. If you are interested in learning from someone, then this may be a good way to find out if your paths are compatible. Even a good shaman may not be suited to you personally. Be prepared to take the time needed to find a way forward. A good friend who is a powerful shaman told me that the teacher will find you when you are ready. We work on ourselves and the universe guides us to where we need to be. I am always suspicious of weekend courses which promise to turn someone into an instant healer /shaman/counsellor with a nice shiny certificate.

What we know of the early religious practices of mankind is based largely on cave paintings and a few archaeological discoveries. Most anthropologists base their conjectures loosely on the tribal cultures which still existed in remote places up until quite recently, - before becoming overrun by modern society.

It is widely believed that shamans have existed as a separate class for at least 30,000 years.

It is my own belief that many men who were unsuited to hunting became shamans. In many ways, their initiation was as tough as that of the warriors in many cultures. Often they were buried for several days to symbolise a journey to the underworld.

Those with minor disabilities which would have made them unfit for hunting were able to help their tribe by performing rituals for success and journeying inward to help find the best places to hunt for game. They would then be on hand to protect the camp during the hunt and use divination to resolve any disputes. Contacting the ancestors may have been an important part of their duties and healing diseases by the use of herbs, and in serious cases, 'soul retrieval'

In soul retrieval, the shaman enters the underworld to find the lost soul of a tribal member. The afflicted may have a mental illness or a fever or be near death.

The shaman must be confident and courageous, or he too may become lost in the vast realms of the underworld and perhaps never return.

I would find this idea quaint, - apart from having witnessed the effects on what could easily be called "loss of soul" on a good friend. He became lost during a badly constructed ritual for past life journeying which was popular in the 1970's. Something rather nasty returned in his stead.

It took most of the night to evict the 'entity' and return this young man and he was never quite the same again. I am aware of the theory of disassociated personality complexes, but it is hard to call them that when they read minds and try to tear your throat out. This is why it is best to get a teacher before tackling more advanced work. Always set your boundaries and your intent. Use whatever help is available to you and meditate in a safe and a sane way. Take things slowly and easily.

My own ideas on how early shamanism was structured, are based more on my own experiences than on the little that is known of early man. Because a group of people may live a nomadic lifestyle or exist in buildings suited to their locality, made of straw and mud, - it hardly proves that their culture has not advanced in 30.000 years.

In 1980, I went to see a small collection of artefacts, taken from Newgrange, Ireland, which were on display in a private library in Dublin. I went with a friend, who I will call Susan. We were invited to go there by the leader of a Rosicrucian group we were involved in. All we were told was to look for an item listed as a ceremonial mace head and see what connection we could make with the object. It was an egg-shaped stone with spiral patterns and a hole through it, large enough to fill a man's hand.

As I gazed at the object, I found myself back in Newgrange, sometime around the building of the passage tomb. A young man dressed in furs sat in front of a fire using the object to grind something in a bowl. He had a clubbed foot. When I commented on it, he laughed and told me it was why he was chosen to be a shaman. When I compared notes with Susan, it turned out that we had shared the same experience. Our accounts of the vision matched perfectly. Oddly, I forgot about this experience for many years until the memory came back to me one day. I wrote the poem below to remind myself of the journey.

Trance is a powerful tool for spiritual exploration.

It can be triggered by many methods.

Hypnotism is the least trustworthy and most dangerous method.

Wounded Heart

Do only fools and cripples live in longing for the light?

Are wounded hearts the only ones who venture deep into the dark to draw aside the veil?

They, who wander aimlessly in woods and fields, to search for wisdom long before the dawn,

Have pity for the poets and the artists who have felt this sense of exile since the day that they were born.

A simple, egg-shaped stone, small enough to fit inside my palm, became the key.

I gazed upon the spirals on this artefact and little did I realise the tale it had to tell.

My friend and I transported back in space and time to when it last was used.

At Newgrange barrow, we both stood, amazed, astounded and bemused.

The shaman sat before a fire, with robes of fur, and mischief in his eyes.

Grinding herbs with stone and bowl, our sudden apparitions seemed to cause him no surprise.

It happened forty, and five thousand years ago, I scarce remember all he had to say.

But one thing stood so clearly in my mind, it stayed with me until this very day.

He seemed quite young for one so wise, with a boyish face and long dark hair,

But, when I gazed upon his crippled foot, he quickly picked up on my stare.

I commented upon the injury at which he saw me glance,

He laughed as if I was a clumsy child, and asked how else would he have had his chance?

The wounded walk the lonely path, and fools rush in where angels fear to tread.

The blind can see the things which normally are hidden by the light, - their vision knows no end.

The beggar and the vagabond have riches that a king will never know.

And when the journey has no maps or charts, the child within us knows which way to go.

Chapter 9

Candle Meditation

Candle meditation and candle 'magic' have a wide application in modern paganism.

There are many variations on this method. One can use different colour candles to focus on different aspects of our life and our intention. There are many 'tables of correspondences' which link various coloured candles to different intentions. The most effective colour correspondences are to be found in any book on colour psychology.

For example, focusing on the colour red will raise our blood pressure, and perhaps, help to build our determination for a particular task.

Red is the colour of action and passion. Try wearing red if you feel a little fatigued or in need of a boost of energy. It works!

Again, we are building rapport with our subconscious minds through the effect of symbols.

White is the colour of purity, meditating on a white candles helps us to gain clarity, and to focus on higher ideals. Mix it with red and you get pink.

Pink is considered by many to be the colour of love. For those who wish to practise candle 'magic', I would simply say that I have never known a love spell that worked unless the person intended already had fond feelings, - except perhaps to focus the feelings and confidence of the person meditating on the candle!

Dark blue is the colour of peace and calm, of night and rest. It is soothing to the mind and brings restfulness and sleep.

Yellow is the colour of the intellect, of enquiry and expansiveness. The researcher and the explorer are very much under the influence of vibrational yellow.

Violet is considered the colour of the spiritual minded the imaginative and the ethereal.

Turquoise (blue-green) is the colour of healing, acquisition and maintaining personal boundaries.

Magic is happening all the time. It is the flow of energy between our total selves and the universe.

Colour is the simplest way to effect beneficial changes by manipulating our moods and desires.

Meditating on the various colours has a marked effect on our moods. Surrounding ourselves with bright vibrant colours helps us become more cheerful and energetic. Cool, soft colours, such as blues and green help us become calmer. Many hospitals have changed their décor based on the discoveries of colour psychology. I believe that the tables of correspondences are most likely based on an intuitive understanding of these principles. As we tune into our own inner worlds, - this wisdom and knowledge become available to us in dreams, visions and sudden inspirations.

In the Kabbala, the candle is a symbol of the four worlds,- Aziluth (fire), Beriah (air), Yesirah (liquid, water), and Assiyah (the physical, the earth) The wick is considered to be the fifth element, Ether,- or the path that links all the worlds from the base of Assiyah to the crown of Aziluth.

For this exercise, use a white candle in a secure candle holder.

Sit at a comfortable distance from the candle.

As you begin the breathing exercise, take time to think about the candle as a gateway to the higher worlds.

Think about the wax, melting into a liquid and flowing up the wick.

The fire which melts the candle turns the liquid into a gas and ignites it, creating more flame.

Like the cycle of spiritual energy which flows into the matrix of the universe and flows back upwards to its source.

See the candle as a point of focus for divine energy.

See the energy flowing out and creating a circle of light which expands to surround you.

Allow your eyes to close and visualise your self-being drawn to travel through the flame back to its divine source.

Allow them to open slowly and focus on the candle again.

See the light open into a protective sphere all around you.

As they grow tired, allow your eyes to close, and repeat the exercise.

Imagine yourself drawn through the flame into the higher worlds.

Take note of any feelings, sensations, memories, images and write them down later.

When you are ready, return through the flame and open your eyes.

Thank any helpers or guides that you may have and absorb the circle, creating a fine mesh of golden light around you.

After practising the meditations for a while, you will begin to have full, detailed journeys.

Always remember that you can open your eyes at any time if they are making you uncomfortable.

Try to always have a drink and a small snack after journeying.

Candle Magic, - Colour Magic

I have avoided the rather thorny subject of magic up to now, - mainly because there has been more waffle and downright lies written about it, than about almost any other subject.

Do I believe in magic? A better question would be, "Do I even know what it is?"

After 45 years of study, I do have some theories. However, this book is too short to cover more than a few basic questions. One neither needs to believe nor disbelieve, in the existence of other worlds for the exercises in this book to work well for them.

Let us start with my favourite quotation from Aleister Crowley, "Magick is the ability to make changes, in conformity with will".

I would say that Magic is the ability to make to make changes in consciousness at will."

How we see the world around us has a huge control over our feelings, actions, and inevitably, our future and our happiness.

We hallucinate all the time. We imagine attitudes and feelings in others that are in fact projections from our own unconscious self-images. Because we are unaware of the true source of our feelings, we live our lives in a random unbalanced way.

Sigmund Freud believed that the subconscious mind was a garbage bin for all the things we cannot face in our lives, and he was partially right.

Carl Jung opened up the possibility that beyond the personal images contained in the unconscious mind, there is a vast fund of helpful imagery to be discovered, which will help us make more sense of our lives and feelings. Our ancestors intuitively tapped into this reservoir and used it to help make useful decisions and live in a balanced harmonious way. Many believe that this gave them a deeper connection with nature and helped in finding food and timing planting and harvesting, but that is for the reader to decide for themselves.

I believe that by gaining rapport with our unconscious minds we can free ourselves from many unexamined beliefs that hold us back from happiness and success.

In a nutshell, meditation gives us a way to reach beyond our habitual way of thinking. We discover symbols during meditation which help us, on reflection, to gain rapport with our own inner worlds.

By reflecting on these symbols, we can begin to slowly unravel the threads of our unconscious impulses and beliefs. These beliefs have remained unexamined because of the non-literate form in which they exist. Our most important and far-reaching opinions about the world around us were formed before we had developed language. This mirrors our development as a species and gives us a link to our distant ancestors who lived in natural harmony with the world around them.

Language brought many advantages for our ancestors, - as it does for the individual. But it comes with the cost of division and disassociation. As we developed language, we learned to assign new meaning to the world around us, while, at the same time, our culture imposed its own particular set of standards upon us.

Magic and ritual attempt to communicate with this non-verbal part of consciousness and to understand the meaning of the communications which we receive in dreams visions and intuition. Poetry and art attempt to express the contents of these inspirations, as do dance, music and mime.

Magic offers us symbols to spur our unconscious minds to cooperate in our efforts to succeed in life. Unfortunately, with magic, we are usually asked to adopt someone else's symbols and try to force them upon ourselves in a one size fits all approach. I would recommend that anyone who wishes to make immediate positive changes in their lives to use colour meditation/magic as a starting point. Refer to the basic colour associations above to begin. Wear the colours in your clothing, - or decorate a room in the colours that apply to the change you wish to obtain. Coloured cloths are an easy way to begin.

The effects are pretty much immediately evident. They will help to build confidence in the work that you are doing.

In my own Celtic culture, magic and mysticism were considered to be very much the province of the bard.

In the magical revival of the late 1800's, it was again the poets and the artists who were the chief motivating forces. In the pages that follow, Bill and I will offer the reader a selection of emotive and mystical art and poetry based on various themes. We have found that the chosen works resonated with many people and helped them to get in touch with their own inner worlds and symbols. As blocked and hidden energies are released, you may well experience tears or laughter. This is nothing to worry about as it merely shows that your meditation has been effective.

Barefoot Angel

You are my light in this dark time,

My one true friend,

My hope of better things to come.

Your laughter is the sparkling bell,

That lifts my failing spirits with its chime,

Making heaven where there once was hell.

You are the sun that makes my shadow tall,

the rock on which I stand

without you, there is no one at all.

You are my life, my day, my night,

each hour, each minute aches for you,

You are the star that makes my evening bright.

You are the shining jewel in the flower.

the full bright moon that lights my darkest hour,

My Princess in her shining tower.

I never thought that I'd know joy again,

until I saw the love in your blue eyes,

and found myself reborn.

Chapter 10

. Seeking our inner child

In a world that has become very materialistic and stressful, many of us love to escape to childhood by watching one of the many fantasy films that are now so popular. For a little while, we can be transported back to a world of childish delight, as disbelief is suspended. That child still lives inside us and has much to offer. In that world of dragons and knights, of elves and faeries, lies a gateway to increased optimism and energy. We can learn to see the world in a fresh new light. Life is truly an adventure if we choose to see it as one.

It is a two-way process. By getting in touch with our inner child, we can unlock a source of creativity and enthusiasm, and learn to see the world as a place of fun and excitement again. We also bring the wisdom gathered from experience to bear, on previously unexamined, childhood beliefs. By doing this we can face old fears and forgotten assumptions that are holding us back in our efforts to build a happy and successful life.

Simply take a few breaths and relax, read the poem and take some time to gaze at the artwork. Then let any sensations or images flow through your mind without judgement. If you wish, then continue the exercise with one of the meditations.

I Remember Me

I remember me,

Suddenly, as plain as plain can be,

I see the world as clear as childlike eyes can see,

and I am young again.

Once more. I see the world is fresh and new,

and filled with wonder and amazing things to do.

Spider webs that sparkle with the sunlit dew,

and I am young again.

The colours of the garden fill my eyes,

Cool green grass, the warm sun flashing rainbows in my eyes,

The fluffy clouds that drift across the pale blue skies,

and I am young again.

What shall I do with this; - my rediscovered youth,

Shall I find a net and hunt for butterflies or newts,

Or shall I sit here in my quiet place, - it matters not,

for I am young again.

I remember me,

And all I ever was is here; - All in life that I held dear,

All that I have ever shared in love has never left,

And I can see it now,

And I am young again.

Chapter 11.

Finding Joy

Only the most unfortunate among us will not have at least one memory of feeling safe and protected. The very fact that we have survived to this stage in our lives and we are reading this book, assures us that we were kept warm, and fed at those times in our lives when we were at our most vulnerable. All of us can fall into the pit of despair, where we feel unloved and unwanted. Use this meditation as a reminder that we have known love and protection and that it is still around us. We carry it in, sometimes forgotten, memories. They may be buried deep in our subconscious, but they are there as a resource. We can tap into them to make our lives more content and filled with joy, or as a buttress against harder times.

Remember that before we can find joy in our lives, we must first find acceptance. It is in acceptance of our situation that we can relax enough to find viable solutions to the challenges which life brings to us. Acceptance brings calmness to our minds and emotions and allows clear thinking. There will be situations which we cannot change immediately. These situations will be easier to adapt to, once we have accepted the truth of our own part in the situations around us. Accepting that our point of view is as valid as the views of those around us is an important step. Looking for the best outcome for all concerned will free us to act in our own best interest without guilt. We are entitled to be happy. We are entitled to feel fulfilled in our lives and to be appreciated. If our needs are not being met by our present situation in life, then we must accept this and plan to move forward. This may require patience and perseverance, but, in accepting the truth of our situation, and doing whatever we can to improve things, we have made the important first step towards calmness and joy.

Breathe deeply and relax. Read the poem and gaze at the picture. Allow your mind to wander. As you begin to meditate, ask your higher self or subconscious mind to guide you to those happy memories. Ask that these feelings of calmness will return to you as soon as it is possible. Remind yourself that life moves in cycles, - from dark to light and that happiness may only be a heartbeat away.

Walk with Me

Leave your nagging doubts behind and walk with me to find some quiet place.

When the glamour of the life you thought you'd love has gone.

When the worries and the stresses get too much.

When you've gone along the road as far as you can go,

When you learned to doubts the things that used to mean so much.

Then walk with me.

Leave the noise behind,

Leave your watch behind and leave your mobile phone.

Find a place where you can truly be alone,

And find me waiting there.

Forest, field or quiet garden.

Beach or park, or just a candle in a quiet room

You will find me in the silence,

Stop and listen, Find the light behind the gloom,

And you will find me there.

You wonder who I am.

I am the gentle touch upon your hair.

I am the comfort and companionship when there is no one there.

I am the eagle flying high, I am the wolf, I am the bear.

I am the Dawning and the End of Time.

Look within yourself, and I am always there.

Life is a journey, but it is also a dance.

Every moment and every action have a meaning and a beauty of their own.

Chapter 12.

The Journey

Building a relationship with our inner selves

Much of the rest of this book will be about meditations to help us gain a more balanced stance towards the most common causes of stress in our lives. However, the foremost intention of meditation has always been to develop a relationship with our inner, or higher, selves. Carl Jung called it the Sacred Marriage, - the life-long attempt to gain full rapport between our Ego and our unconscious minds. One may see this as a spiritual journey, or as a psychological journey,-it matters little to the endeavour of finding our own pathway through life. Many who take this journey will be spurred on by past trauma. Even if you are not aware of any past incidents which may be at the root of your search, keep this in mind. Always proceed slowly and carefully. Find and use any help groups or trustworthy advisors available to you.

Enjoy this voyage of discovery. You will find many resources that you never expected within yourself. Life will open up many new opportunities as you open up your own mind and see the possibilities. Relaxation and meditation are the pathways to finding a new calmness and self-confidence. As we deal with hidden fears, we will begin to achieve things that we once thought impossible for us. I can testify to this from my own experience. Remember, to explore the inner worlds is to explore a world of magic and symbolism. The archetypes appear to us in the form of ancient gods and goddesses, in signs and symbols. It is our own individual reactions to these inner energies that count. It is here that we find our own way forward. Relax, read the poem and gaze at the artwork. Your journey has truly begun.

The Sacred Marriage.

The Lord and Lady glide about the forest, as the softly sighing leaves are whispering in the silver light.

The dwellers of the woods are quiet and still, and dark eyes gaze upon the scene entranced,

No man, nor beast would dare disturb the ritual of this night.

Above, the Goddess lights her emissaries, as the moon and earth enjoin in Sacred Dance.

Tall and stately like a silver birch, the Lady flows like liquid moonlight through the trees,

Laughter, like the tinkling of a golden bell, caresses sensual lips and flutters off into the waiting night.

Great Pan himself, is so enamoured of her beauty that he pauses in his play, to place a kiss upon her knee,

Then He resumes His Dance and placing pipe to lips, He fills the Still night air with merriment and pure delight.

Fire to speed the coming of the Sun, blazing high, as sparks are flying to the sky.

Warm the Earth!

Writhe like new-grown saplings reaching to the light!

Naked feet, caressing and cajoling Mother earth, can feel Her Spirit and Her Power rise,

And Spring is surely hastened with the coming of Her Lover, at sunrise.

My journey has but just begun, I cannot tell this tale in full.

Perhaps my senses are too numb, perhaps my mind to dull.

But every day I ask the Gods of fire that I may wake,

and every night I look up to the Moon for guidance,

on the journeys, I may make.

Chapter 13.

Challenging Times.

I have known people with unshakeable confidence, people who have merrily gone from disaster to disaster with no realisation of the chaos they sow on their journey through life. Fortunately, not too many of us suffer from this form of megalomania. Most of us struggle with self-doubt and judge ourselves too harshly, for what are common human failings. Also, the temptation is always there, to push the blame onto others as a way of easing our own feelings. The only balanced way of dealing with difficult situations is by acting with honesty and compassion.

We need to accept that we do not have full control over the consequences of our actions, - only over our intentions. We have nothing to reprimand ourselves for, if we acted in good faith, based on the knowledge available to us at the time, - By the same token, we need to take the same approach to the actions of others. Much of what we assume to be the intentions of others is mistaken. Often our assumption is a pointer to our own hidden attitudes and memories. Obviously, we need to protect ourselves and our loved ones, - but, by cultivating an attitude of understanding where possible, we can develop a deeper understanding of our own hidden fears and motivations.

Each one of us will have some form of hidden memory of a time of fear, uncertainty or pain. It may be connected to a look, a sound, a smell or many other possible 'cues'. I use the word 'cue', because just like in a play, - it is a prompt to begin a particular series of feelings or actions. It may even begin with 'signals' in the womb, - due to some trauma experienced by our mother. It may be a deep-seated feeling of abandonment or anxiety, caused by a tired or overtaxed parent missing a feed or nappy change. Any other random sound or sensation may become associated with those feelings of abandonment, and be built on over the years.

Acceptance and compassion for others, allows us to begin the process of self-healing. It reduces our own anxiety and excessive demands on ourselves as well as others. By reviewing past situations in a calm, accepting way, we learn to see the situations with a new honesty and clarity. We can unearth the bedrock of our own personalities and begin to understand why we are likely to behave in the same way in certain circumstances. This frees us to choose to avoid certain scenarios or develop a new more useful attitude or reaction to future similar events. This acceptance and compassion must also be applied to ourselves. We need to constantly remind ourselves that we are worthy of love, joy and prosperity.

Breathe deeply and relax. Allow the images to flow. Follow with one of the meditations if you wish. Write down anything that you remember.

Be Gentle

Be gentle with your heart,

The world can change within a single beat.

Tread lightly in the world,

And treat with kindness, all the people you may meet.

Wisdom costs us dearly,

The price we have to pay, - we pay in sorrow and in loss.

And all the times we try, - we ask ourselves the reason why,

But still, we carry on the burden of survival, for the sake of those we love.

And gaze in silent question at the grey and sullen sky.

Rage against the storms that carry all we love away.

Turn your back against the setting sun that leaves us cold, or hungry or alone at end of day.

Shake your fist and cry out to the moon, - howling out with sorrow like the solitary wolf.

Touch the earth with dewy tears as sunrise makes us face another day.

But still, the earth will turn, and we will heal, - for that is nature's way.

Chapter 14.

Finding Love

Many of us turn to various forms of spirituality, when in fact our true needs might be best met by a dating site or social club. We are a social species and, in our crowded lives and crowded cities, human interaction has become stifled by stress and fear. Those moving to rural areas may find themselves even more isolated due to lack of opportunity, or not having the necessary skills and confidence to break through the barriers of natural reserve and become active members of their new community. Unless we are aware of our own true needs, we may become the willing victims of various cults and groups, sacrificing any hope of real contentment and individuality in return for a sheltered existence among those who would fleece us like sheep!

In dealing with the source of our desire for enlightenment, we are not abandoning spirituality if we decide or discover that what we need first is a family or a dependable circle of friends, - or perhaps even the admiration of those around us! If it is a necessary part of our journey, then true spirituality is not likely to be open to us until we have worked through our needs and desires.

I once gave a tarot reading to a single lady with children. All that came up in the reading were money matters and other events connecting with the raising of her family. She complained, - saying that it was all she ever got from readers and psychics. She wanted to know about her love prospects. I gave her a second in-depth reading, concentrating totally on possible love matters. I described a meeting with someone about 3 months ahead of time. I gave her the place they would meet and a detailed description of the person whom she would come into contact with. Although there was an engagement party invitation for that time, she refused to consider the possibility because the person I described was about 5 years older than her.

There may be many hidden expectations or fears holding us back from full involvement with another person, or our local community. Friends, family, neighbours and colleagues are important to our mental health and happiness. Local events and charities can be a great way to expand our connections and make our lives feel more fulfilled. In today's' overcrowded societies it is all too easy to become isolated and alone. It is important to find ways to reach out to others in an environment which feels safe. Learning a new craft or sharing a hobby is an excellent way to meet like-minded people. Volunteer work can get us out and about and there are also many support groups for those who might find this a daunting step to take. The greatest obstacle to widening our circle of friends and acquaintances is usually our own fears and childhood programming. Use the meditation to begin to open up and explore the possibilities in our imagination. What we can imagine ourselves doing will become a real possibility with time and practice.

Take a few deep breaths, read the poem, spend some time absorbing the images from the artwork. Use any of the meditations in the first pages. After meditation, write down anything you remember for later review.

True love begins when we place the happiness and welfare of another before our own

Limitless Love

Who can put a limit on the way we choose to love

Who can dare to tell us who we choose to share our lives

We may share our hearts and dreams with many or with few,

Only when we listen to our hearts can we be wise,

Then our hearts will tell us what it is that we must do.

None of us can tell if life is going to be long or to be brief.

Love may last a thousand lives or blossom in a single day.

That Life is meant for love is still my uttermost belief,

And if your love is wise or rash, is just for you to say.

For life flies by so fast, and only love can conquer grief.

Grasp the nettle firmly, and hold on tight to all that you hold dear,

Drain the cup of life, don't let you precious minutes drip away.

Don't stop to count the cost of love. Don't live your life in fear,

This day may be your very last, don't wish it all away.

One moment spent in loves embrace can heal the many lonely years.

Chapter 15.

The Muse Awaits

Apart from any observations that may spring into my mind while editing, the next pages of this book will be comprised of various images and poems

We hope that the reader will enjoy these as inspirational art, - as well as using them as stepping stones for meditation. Feel free to write your own work too. Any form of artistic expression will open the doors to healing in many unforeseeable ways. There are so many ways in which we can learn to express those inner energies which are hard to describe in everyday language.

I believe that with a little time and determination. most people will find a channel which suits them, with a little shopping around. Knitting, woodcarving, painting, needlepoint, flower arranging and card making are a few of the many methods of self-expression that are open to us.

I will begin with a tribute to the many new-age philosophies which have brought light and love into my search for spirituality.

It is called Rags and Feathers.

Only by leaving false certainty behind can we find true spirituality.

It is a leap of faith and a determination to trust our own instincts and inner guidance.

Rags and Feathers.

Rags and feathers are the way the children born of Spirit fly today.

We drag our tattered wings of wood and bone beyond the travelled way.

On mountaintops and high-rise blocks, we brace our wings against the breeze.

To fly, or fall, becomes our only prayer, - we will not live our lives on bended knees.

We are children once again, - born once more in ignorance and awe.

We can no longer cling to tablets made of stone or other man-made laws.

Wood and bone, and rags and feathers are our teachers now.

We know, that in the fantasies we weave, the truth will shine, somehow.

Are we certain? We are only certain that this moment is the one that slips away.

This moment is the only chance we have to laugh, to love, to play.

This moment is the pinnacle of truth, this moment is the purpose of our youth.

This moment is the life we have which quickly fades away.

The sun begins to rise as rags and feathers ruffle in the breeze.

The golden glow of morning forms a web of light across the rooftops and the trees.

Will our hopes be dashed upon the ground or lift us far beyond despondence and unease?

It matters little if we fly or fall, - for there is nothing left within our hearts but peace.

The Long Goodbye

Although, sometimes, you can't remember who I am.

The many loving years, the many smiles and tears,

The many joys we shared throughout the happy years,

will never fade from me.

They are written on my heart in gold.

They will not fade as I grow old.

So I can hold your hand and smile,

and I will be your memory for just a little while,

when your own fading memory beguiles

I dread those moments when the light of recognition fails,

It makes me feel that I am all alone, - it makes you look so frail,

My life becomes a prison guard's, - your happy home becomes a jail.

I try to light the love-light in your eyes again, but now and then I fail.

You have not passed away from me,

Although I see your face as if another wears your skin,

I see a frightened child where once I saw my love, my kin.

Sometimes, it's hard to see your spirit shine, from deep behind your pain.

This broken body, stripped of certainty and strength is all that I hold dear,

For you are there my love, behind the panic and confusion and the fear.

Be still, my Love, be calm, for time is fleeting in this vale of tears,

And soon our spirits both will rise, and cast away the troubled years.

Then, we shall be as one again,

Someday

To find magic, we have only to look at the world through the eyes of childhood.

Where did the Magic go?

Where did the magic go?

Is it sleeping underneath the crisp, white snow?

I saw the magic falling from the sky the other night,

As I looked out my window and it filled my mind with innocent delight.

Has the Magic gone away?

I thought I saw it as I walked along the beach the other day.

It was hiding, shyly, in a little spiral shell, I found.

I placed it to my ear and heard the magic of my childhood's happy sounds.

Has the Magic floated far away upon some playful breeze?

I thought I heard it scampering across a woodland floor and tickling the sleepy leaves.

They were whispering and giggling to each other as I slowly sauntered by.

Tucked up warm against the chilly winds, beneath a January sky.

Magic sends its laughter echoing across the many years.

Magic sends its love to take away our sadness and our tears.

Magic brings us many friends and lovers who will make us fight and laugh and play.

Magic is the breath of life which 'wakens with us every blessed day.

The Dark Night of the Soul

When all our dreams are shattered, and all our hopes are lost,

Our shady trees uprooted. Our crops all turned to dust,

What keeps a Lover waiting, when their love is all in vain?

Or keeps the farmer planting when there's little hope of rain?

What is this candle in the dark?

This whisper in the silence,

That keeps us strong when hope is gone,

Renewing hope afresh with each new dawn.

Let Me Go with You.

Let me go with you to where the quiet waters flow by wooded fields that are not owned by man.

To where the music whispers from the sunlit trees and settles on my little raft to soothe my fevered brain.

Where ripened fruit lies heavy on the boughs, and gently drops into my tiny dhow, to fill my hungers need.

That Faery land where I will never have to deal with anger or with greed, - where I need never, ever kill to feed,

Please let me go with you.

Just let me drift along, beside your magic shores, and I will cup my hands and drink my fill,

The waters of forgetfulness will wash the past away and heal my heart of all its ills.

The singing of the birds will raise my spirits higher than their lofty flight,

And when the moon appears, then I will sleep with restful mind this night,

Please let me go with you.

Then just before the mornings crimson light, I will awake, and from my tiny craft, I will alight.

And by the dying embers of your Faery fires, I'll play my pipes and beat my drum for your delight,

Then as you go unto your rest I'll sing a lullaby for you, and I will sing my best, as lovers do.

For if it is your will, I'll lay beside you quiet and still, and we will be together for forever more,

Please let me go with you.

Patrick W Kavanagh

Winter Fae

The winter has been long and cold, and springtime still seems very far away.

I sit here snuggled in the warmth with misty dreams of childhood and the Fae.

How I miss glowing embers, underneath the flaming sods of turf that fed our fire.

When I used to sit in quiet contemplation as the faeries fed my heart's desire.

Dancing gaily through the woodlands, mirrored in the phosphorescent world of smoke and flame.

Faerie troopers marched across the gleaming forests edged with crimson and with gold.

Carriages of purest white, and silver reins upon the coal black shires that proudly cantered by.

Horsemen dressed in silver armour, prancing as they raised their glistening lances to the sky.

Then the Faery Queen, - magnificent in sparkling gown, she turned and waved to me.

Her wings like delicate, translucent butterflies which fluttered blue against the ruby trees.

I cannot think of any other joy as sweet as this, my fondest childhood memory,

Though fifty years have passed since then, it lingers, still as fresh and clear to me.

Every word I place here on the page brings childhood's wonder closer to my mind.

With all the joys and mysteries that, for a little while, I thought that I had left so far behind.

Join me now and let us gaze upon the embers hand in hand with our own inner eyes.

The perhaps we both can sleep, and dream of meadows filled with sprightly flowers,

and cloudless, sunny skies.

The Goddess Smiles.

For many years I've longed to pass beyond that final door,

To where I know, deep in my heart, that we were once before.

Beyond this solitary life among the careless throng,

To where our souls can rest in peace, in that still world where I know we belong.

And yet, sometimes, I hear your sweet angelic voice above the traffics roar.

For one sweet moment, we are hand in hand as once before.

My exile here becomes a heartbeat closer to your smile,

And I am blessed with just a moment's rest from trouble and from toil.

I know that I must wait a while, before I glimpse once more, your healing smile.

Your beauty flows down to us still, through earth and sea and sky.

The burden of this life grows heavy, and the time can pass so slow.

Until that day, when I can be with you, there is no place I really wish to go.

Help me still this longing that is tearing at my heart.

I cannot bear this pain that grips my soul, each day apart.

There is much in this harsh world which I have left to do.

Until, that blessed day, when I am, once again, with you.

Nature teaches without words.

Listening to the whispering of the wind in the trees can lead us to great wisdom.

Weeping Willow

Dreaming underneath the weeping willow tree, there are no tears.

No more gazing back across the lonely years.

No more waiting for the future to unfold.

No more longing for that special person I could hold.

No more wishing, and no more regrets.

I am simply me, and I am all that I can be.

Let the river flow, and let the sorrow go.

It has no place inside my heart and soul.

The rippling of the water soothes my mind.

It drifts along its current as I leave the past behind.

Sunlight flickers through the branches, - rainbow colours soothe my eyes.

Up above, the swans are flying past, through clear blue skies.

How I wish that I could fly with you.

I long to soar, across those skies so blue.

To that sweet land where sorrow has no claim,

A land where trouble does not know my name.

Silence is our greatest teacher

Stillness is the path to wisdom.

Soft Rain in a Summer Garden.

The rain falls softly on the daisy sprinkled, summer grass,

Spreading tiny, sparkling globes of silvery light.

It scatters gentle ripples on the pond,

that just a little while ago was smooth as glass.

And still,l I sit and gaze with lazy eyes at all the beauty,

and at something just beyond my sight.

The smell of dew on earth and leaves and summer flowers,

Distracts me just a little from a reverie

that may have lasted minutes or for many hours.

I cannot tell, I cannot even quite remember what I saw,

But still, I feel the peace, the calmness that it gave to me,

As if I'd glimpsed a land of magic, through an open door.

I cannot bear to leave this place, despite the rain,

So much solace, so much love has filled my heart.

I realise that life is bitter-sweet,

That joy will always come to wash away life's pain.

As once again we raise our heads and make a brand-new start.

Imagination is the key to inner truth

The Mysterious Disappearance of an Imaginary Friend

Feeling lost and bored, I climbed into the apple tree, but did not find you there,

In the crawl-space underneath the house, I found a sleepy little mouse,

a cricket, and a lonely louse,

I looked inside our little lair, but there was neither hide nor hair,

And now I've checked in all our favourite spots, I must admit,

I cannot find you anywhere!

I cannot quite remember when I'd noticed you were gone,

You must have slipped away and never said goodbye,

Thinking back on all the happy summer days we shared,

Knowing what it meant to have a friend who really cared,

I can't believe that when you left, I never even cried.

You were there, for all the times, when no one else came out to play.

We wandered miles, just you and I, to all the magic places and we stayed out unafraid, until the very end of day.

The woods were never dark and lonely, you could tell the names of all the trees,

And we would lie upon the leafy ground and listen to the buzzing of the bees.

The long hot days were spent with all our forest friends, I thought those happy days would never end,

Those days of solitude and ease.

You even spoke to all the birds and they would land beside us,

While butterflies would fly about, and ladybugs would nestle in my hair.

You listened kindly to my every tale of woe,

and helped me do the very things I never thought I'd dare,

You brought me joy and comfort and companionship and trust.

But now I look in all our little places and I cannot find you there.

Meaning

A single feather falls from a clear blue sky,

into your open palm.

Mystery, Truth, Beauty, Love,

The Universe is still and has a meaning of its own.

It simply is.

The busy human mind has spun a web of fantasy and lies.

We trample on the flowers,

But never once look to the skies.

The Ace of Cups

The sun is setting slowly; I understand its dignified resistance to the night.

Softly it descends behind the wintry trees and gently impregnates the pond with golden light.

Just like the ace of cups, an ancient symbol for the dawn of life,

When God made love and gave his essence to his child, the universe.

Wrapped up warm and sitting here just gazing at this scene,

I wander back through time, and all that I have been,

The images fly by in haste, my life was long, there have been quite a few,

But still, the ones which stand out stark and strong are images of you.

The golden light reminds me of your hair, like ripened corn or candles in a quiet church,

I close my eyes and I can see you standing there, and I can almost feel your gentle touch.

I smell your scent, it's carried on the winter's breeze, you're not so very far away,

Sometimes I can't believe that your still here, my angel and my comfort in these fading days.

I don't feel very sad, this life of mine was precious and I've had my fill of tears and joy,

And I have had my share of undeserved love, much more than I imagined as a boy.

Those childish dreams of fame and wanton lust, have all returned to ignorance and dust,

I've had much greater treasures in my life, my families, my homes, my wife,

And I will sleep in peace.

Spirit is always reaching out to us.

The Goddess Calls

Who are you?

What is this new longing which has crept into my restful soul?

I hear your quiet whisper, but, in words not of my race.

There is nothing in this world is seek, - My cup is full

and yet, you tempt me. Calling softly from some distant place.

Are you the whisper in the wind that calls my name?

Perhaps you are the breaking of the waves against some rocky shore?

Or Moonlit shadows rustling in some country lane.

I feel as ...if somehow, you've called my name before.

Stay! Don't fade away!

Your gentle torture seems to stir my bones.

I wait and listen in this dying light of day,

Perhaps My Goddess speaks in these soft tones.

Oh, how I wish that I were not so deaf and blind

to all those things on which my spirit soars,

That all the thoughts which cloud my mind were gone,

And only You and I remained as once before.

The Dawn

A peaceful Stillness in the early morning rain,

The world is sleeping; lost within its dreams, divine,

A quiet moment, silent, soft, without a hint of joy or pain,

No past, no future beckons, - This moment, - truly mine.

The placid waters of a quiet lake are my domain.

I rest my mind and I await the workings of my fate,

But Calmness still Remains,

And I am simply me.

The day shall bring what it may bring,

And I shall simply "Be".

So Many Worlds in One

There are so many worlds in one.

Maybe, in some far-off time, they will return to where they've first begun.

Spirit flies beyond the bounds of space and time,

The past, the present and the future beat within a single endless rhyme.

The poet and the prophet speak with just one single voice.

We listen to their ramblings and their ravings, for we sense they have no choice.

They only say the things they hear, and try to show the things they see.

But neither they nor we can truly understand until our egos cease to be.

Yet the world we know is sometimes kind,

And the worlds beyond this world can heal the heart and mind.

If we open up our eyes and see the vastness of eternity,

It's there in front of us if we could only stop the world, and simply be.

Death is simply a doorway to other worlds.

Whispers from a Distant Shore.

I know we only had a little while,

But now the end has come and gone, I have to say,

You made me cry a lot less than you made me smile.

So, don't be sad for me,

just shed your tears and say goodbye,

Our time is over you and I,

at least until we meet on some far shore, someday.

Be glad for me, I have no pain,

Except for sadness every time I see you cry.

How I dread the answers that I cannot give,

Each time you ask the reason why.

You must accept that it is over now, and all my time is spent,

at least until the day, I must return.

And you must learn to live your life and be content.

Another writes these words for me, to tell you all I need to let you know,

The many things I need to say, and all the things that I forgot to show.

Although you think that I am far away, I watch you every day,

Be still, and listen, for my voice is very faint.

And Know, I love you and I always will,

and we will be together soon enough.

So take the cup of joy in both your hands and drink your fill,

if not for you, then do this thing for me,

and I will rest in peace.

Whispers in The Early Morning Hours

Whispers in the early morning hours,

Soft as petals falling on the dewy grass,

I lay upon the cool, damp earth,

Eyes closed, I feel the rising sun,

the Earth and I are one,

And peace is mine at last.

No more the taunting, haunting echoes of the past,

I will honour all that was, and say goodbye.

No more the clinging ivy of those distant days,

I feel them fading like the summer haze,

when evening falls and spreads the mantle of the night.

Then I will gently call and say goodnight

to all my tears and all my fears.

The goddess calls me softly to her side,

And I will sleep in peace this night.

The days will flow and happy times will come and go.

It is the way of life.

And I will live in gratitude for all I have and all that was,

and though I never will forget,

I'll take the time each day, to count the many blessings I have known,

and When my time has passed, and I must leave this life,

There will be no regret,

I will think of all those lovely people who have shared my life,

And I will rest in peace.

Landscapes

Enough of sadness let us talk of things that fill the heart with Joy!

Let us fill these last few wintry days with all the memories of what we did as girls and boys.

Raise your spirits! Raise your glass, - spring was late in coming but it's here at last,

And soon the last few snowy fields will thaw to show that the winters passed.

Climbing trees and wounded knees, kisses were enough to take the momentary pain away.

Long hot summers filled with silly rhymes and earnest play.

Simple Simon said, and we all simply did the simple joyful things that children did,

And summer seems to stretch forever in my memory of when I was a kid.

A piece of string, the source of so much fun, a stick and paper added made a kite that flew up to the sun,

A bow and arrow that could barely fly, but still it made us into warriors, and when we went to war, our mother's saucepan was a drum.

Skipping ropes and skipping school. Skipping stones across a pool,

Chasing all around the grass and getting thrown out of the park because we played the fool.

Dolls of rags, and shopping bags. Plastic toys and little trinkets when the rag-man came our way.

Saving jars and bottles for the trade, and innocently thrilled with all the deals we'd make that day.

Meeting up in all the secret hideaways we made and creeping through the jungle just a hundred yards from home,

Cowboys and Indians, with pistols made of wood, and high tea under tables with coffee made of mud,

and sullen dolls that made you think of that far-off and fateful day when you have children of your own.

And with that thought, the summers flew away and left me as I am today,

But the winters! Oh, what fun, virgins fields and virgin footprints where we run.

Snowmen and snowball fights. We slide on pavements with our breadboard sleighs,

Clear and starry nights, then sunlit frosty mornings, followed by the cold, crisp days.

In my mind, my childhood days are just a dream away.

Endless Journey

Drifting, floating, warm sun on my skin, the gentle lapping of the river soothes my wandering mind,

A summer breeze sends fluffy clouds across a pale blue sky that scarcely shades the sun.

Along the banks, a host of white and yellow flowers softly, mutely tell me to unwind,

To leave my cares and woes behind and wallow in their beauty and their scent until this blessed day is done.

I rest my head upon my coat and savour every moment of this restful day,

Lying, dozing, drifting in my tiny, rented skiff, which barely fits from end to end,

The rivers mine for just one day, the singing of the birds just seems to say,

Just rest a while, our little friend, as if the beauty of this day may never end.

Paddles overboard, the rudder long ignored, I lie in reverie and drift down to the open sea,

Idly wondering if I drift for long enough, my little skiff may take me to eternity,

Or will I simply drift ashore and start anew, - just simply be a different me,

Another day, another life, another world, - another way to be.

Childhood Friends

I whistled as I rambled slowly down the woodland path in June.

The sunlight trickled through the trees and flickered through the leafy gloom.

I breathed deeply as the many forest scents assailed my senses, - filling me with joy.

The memories flooded back, and once again, I was a little boy.

I see you! - even though you blend into the trees just as you did so many years ago.

You giggle as you hide and once again my heart feels childish glee.

Just as it did when I was very young and played here all alone

Until that first amazing day, I caught you sneaking up on me.

We had no words, except the ones I made up in my mind.

But still, you were the greatest friend a child could ever find.

Peer and sneak, and hide and seek we stalked each other every day.

It broke my heart that awful day my parents said we had to move away.

We sat in silence as my tears poured down and made my poor eyes burn.

I made a promise that someday, somehow, when I was older, I'd return.

So many years have passed. I am ashamed to say, that I forgot you for a while.

But though I can no longer see you plain- I sense your welcome smile.

You touch my mind so gently, and finally, I see your wings of gossamer and lace.

My heart is fit to burst with joy as finally, I see your pretty face.

My beaming smile turns into laughter as I see your little friends appear.

From under every leaf and rock, a hundred tiny faces start to peer.

You gently touch my hand and I began to glow.

I felt my tiny wings appear, just as they did so many years ago.

Face to face and eye to eye, - you held me close as both of us begin to fly.

I look back once to where my crumpled body lies upon the ground,

and as we fly away to Sidhe, I say one last goodbye.

The Song of White Swan Flying

It is a good day to die,

I shall proudly hold my head up high, beneath my father in the sky.

and I shall stand and fight this day, although it is my last.

I will no longer fear the future, neither will I mourn the past.

My feet are firm upon my mother's earth,

and reaching down I take a pinch of sacred dirt,

My father's dust shall be the paint I wear this final day.

And I will die before I let them drag me far away.

This is my land,

And here is where I make my stand,

It's bounty I have shared with kin of scale and skin and fur,

There are no tears left in this broken heart, and I shall weep no more.

I shall not leave this place,

I shall not live in misery and in disgrace.

My ancestors and I will sit and talk this night,

Then I will pour my blood upon the earth before the dying of the light.

And now I mount my horse and ride into the roar of many guns,

See how her flanks are painted with my palms and red with my own blood.

We helped them in their hour of need and now behind the guns, I see them stood,-

The children of the children, whom the parents of my parents, should have shunned.

The sky has opened, and my father softly calls my name,

"Take heart, my son, our time has passed, but it will come again"

One day the buffalo will fill the land again, and we will feast and live in peace,

White Buffalo will come, and all four colours of mankind unite and heal the Earth again.

I will weep no more.

I Am Ready to Leave.

I am ready to leave, for the fear has passed, and there is nothing left to prove,

I am ready to leave, the time has long already past, for all that binds me here.

I am ready to leave, the knots that held me have all frayed, they lie in tattered shreds about my feet.

I am ready to leave, the nails that pinned me to this tree,

have long since rusted back to dust,

And I am free.

My burdens cease to bother me; their weight has stripped my nerves of pain,

My burdens soon will find another beast to carry them, when I have gone away.

Responsibility lies lightly on my brow, I care not what they do or say, my time is over, anyway.

It's just the fear of coming back, that keeps me here today,

but still, my time to leave has come,

No matter what you say.

My time to leave has come.

Let the bailiff knock upon my door, tell that he missed me, he is far too late.

Let the hounds of Fate come baying at my gate,

Their howling doesn't bother me at all, I've washed away the writing on the wall,

Let some other take the fall,

My time to leave is here,

but I'll be watching,

and I will be deeply touched,

If you should shed a tear.

It always ends too soon,
The dancing of the butterfly, - the rising of the moon.
But, there are other worlds where time holds little sway.
And, somewhere in those worlds, I know that you and I will meet again someday.

The Shining Path

Sit beside me love and let me hear you sing once more.

The road ahead is calling; I can see the open door.

When I close my eyes, I see it stretching out into the endless night,-

A silver path between the trees that glow with mystic light.

Trying not to breathe too deep, I catch the scent of orchids in the calm night air.

And, though I feel your hand in mine, in many ways I am already there.

Underneath the smiling moon, whose halo spreads across the shimmering sky.

The twinkling stars illuminate the wispy clouds that slowly wander by.

What a peaceful night to pass into the glory that beyond the heavens lies.

Although I hate to leave, there is a light of wonder in my dimming eyes.

As I slowly drift beyond the reach of all the joys and all the sorrows of the day.

I feel your final kiss upon my lips and gently slip away.

Do not cry for me, my love. A perfect passing crowned my life with bliss.

I will always have my time with you and I will always tremble at that final kiss.

Should it pass that I must face, once more, this world of beauty, fear and pain.

I know the fates will draw us to each other, and, one day,

I'll I hold you to my breast again.

Always look to the child within to guide us to lasting happiness

You are free,

Free as the wind that weaves and billows as it dances with the ripening corn.

You are strong,

Stronger than the sun which lifts the waters of this world with just a fleeting glance.

You are ancient,

Older than the Universe in which this tiny planet spins to give us night and morn.

You are young,

Born again each lifetime, as your spirit throws the dice of life and joins in with the dance.

We are sleeping,

I believe that one day we will waken, to become all we may be.

We are children,

So let us children, view the world again with child-like eyes.

We are one,

We are on with all that was, and all that is, and what will ever be.

We have fallen,

We have fallen for a little while, until the day when one by one, we rise.

Rise each day,

Rise each day and hear the morning chorus fill the air with simple joy.

Find a way,

Find a way to see the best in all the gifts and Challenges that nature brings.

See the path,

See the path ahead is measured out to test, but never to exceed what we can bear.

Live in love, Live in love, and soon the love in which you live will bring you all the gifts that only Love can bring.

Breathe in peace… Breathe out tension

Breathe in love… Breathe out fear

Breathe in Joy… Breathe out sorrow

Change in a World of Restrictions.

We plod along the paths set out by those who love and wish to keep us, safe.

Family. Our greatest strength, our greatest trial,

Extend their loving arms and keep us on the travelled way.

We must keep to the rules; we mustn't play the fool,

They fear that we might travel far away,

And not return.

Fear our guide, and hidden shames, - the goads that drive us on,

What if people realise that we are not the same?

What if they should wipe away our budding life with sermons, or with stones?

Perhaps electric shock, or drugs, or walk away and leave us all alone.

At least, they may not burn us at the stake and crush and stretch our bones.

The masters say that we have much more freedom now,-

The freedom of the herd, the freedom to be never left alone,

If we obey.

Ask the oldest Tree that you can find, and He will show you how to clear your mind,

Ask the Fox, the Badger, - They are masters of the hidden way.

Ask the Vole, the Stoat, the Ferret, - Open up your heart to love.

They will teach you how to open up to all the Goddess has to say.

Then you can change this very moment,

You can build a better life today.

And then you will be truly free.

If you feel anxious or unable to cope, the best immediate solution is to take a long walk.

A walk in the woods is the best cure for many of life's stresses.

Chapter 16.

About the Author

Vancouver artist Bill Oliver has had a deep lifetime interest in the paranormal and his earlier artwork reflected these interests. As his artwork progressed, he found himself drawn away from the paranormal and towards the world of Celtic myth and legend. This has led him to a further and deeper relation and understanding of his own ancestry and a collective consciousness. With family lineage deeply rooted in Ireland, Scotland, and England, he now draws from the deep well of the traditions and lore of ancient Celtic culture and ancestral memories.

Writer, poet, Patrick W Kavanagh was born in Dublin and now lives and works in Lincolnshire in a small rural town. Patrick became fascinated by the strange abilities of the human mind from watching his mother give psychic readings using tea-leaves and playing cards. With a lifelong interest in metaphysics and parapsychology, he has given tarot and spirit readings for over 40 years. He travels to many events with his wife Tina, exploring the power of shamanic drumming to heal, and induce therapeutic trance states. They also hold a regular drumming circle in the picturesque Lincolnshire Wolds.

Bill and Patrick came into contact through the intervention of a well-known Psychic, Eileen Akrill, from North Cave in Yorkshire. Mrs Akrill insisted that Patrick should contact Bill, on the advice of her spirit guide. After several weeks of constant reminders from Eileen, Patrick viewed Bills page and was immediately captivated by his stunning artwork. He sent him a sample to match a published picture.

Bill found in Patrick's poetry and prose, a perfect complement to the inspiration behind his art.

After several trial pieces were sent back and forth across the Atlantic, which was a perfect match without any consultation, - 'From the Muse' was born.

Also available at most retailers by Patrick W Kavanagh

Kiara

Distant Shores

From the Muse